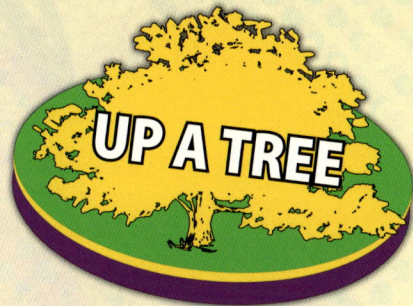

Flying Lemurs

Willow Clark

PowerKiDS
press.

New York

Published in 2012 by The Rosen Publishing Group, Inc.
29 East 21st Street, New York, NY 10010

First Edition

Editor: Joanne Randolph
Book Design: Greg Tucker
Layout Design: Ashley Drago

Photo Credits: Cover (main, background), pp. 10, 18, 22 Shutterstock.com; pp. 4–5, 11, 16 (bottom) Tim (or Timothy) Laman/National Geographic/Getty Images; p. 6 C. S. Ling/Getty Images; pp. 8, 9, 14, 19, 20 © Azmi Bogart; pp. 12–13, 17 © NHPA/SuperStock; pp. 15, 21 Mattias Klum/ National Geographic/Getty Images; p. 16 (left) © www.iStockphoto.com/Hannes Schleicher.

Library of Congress Cataloging-in-Publication Data

Clark, Willow.
  Flying lemurs / by Willow Clark. — 1st ed.
     p. cm. — (Up a tree)
  Includes index.
  ISBN 978-1-4488-6184-2 (library binding) — ISBN 978-1-4488-6327-3 (pbk.) —
ISBN 978-1-4488-6328-0 (6-pack)
  1. Flying lemurs—Juvenile literature. I. Title.
  QL737.D4C53 2012
  599.33—dc23
                            2011027087

Manufactured in the United States of America

CPSIA Compliance Information: Batch #WW12PK: For Further Information contact Rosen Publishing, New York, New York at 1-800-237-9932

Contents

What's in a Name?

The flying lemur, or colugo, is an animal that almost never leaves the trees in which it lives. These small, shy **mammals** are most commonly seen flying through the air as they move between trees.

Even though they are called flying lemurs, colugos cannot fly. Instead they glide like kites, using the skin that connects their front and back legs to keep them in the air. Colugos are not really lemurs, either. They are called lemurs because their faces look like lemurs' faces. True lemurs live in Madagascar, an island in the Indian Ocean. Flying lemurs live in Southeast Asia.

Colugos are about the size of a large squirrel. They often hang under branches rather than sitting on top of them.

At Home in the Trees

There are two **species** of flying lemurs. Both species live in Southeast Asia. The Philippine flying lemur lives in the Philippines. The Sunda flying lemur lives in Thailand, Indonesia, Malaysia, Borneo, Singapore, and Myanmar.

Colugos have long arms and legs. Their front legs and back legs are about the same length.

Both kinds of flying lemurs are **arboreal**, meaning they live in trees. Just about everything they need is found

CHINA

VIETNAM

PHILIPPINES

Philippine Sea

MALAYSIA

Indian Ocean

INDONESIA

MAP KEY

Philippine Lemur Range

Sunda Lemur Range

in the treetops of the **tropical** rain forest **habitats** in which they live. Flying lemurs are **nocturnal**. This means they are active mostly at night.

7

The Two Colugos

Well-known animals that are most closely related to flying lemurs include tree shrews and **primates**. Primates are animals such as lemurs and monkeys. Colugos are not tree shrews or primates, though. They belong to an order called Dermoptera.

This is a Sunda flying lemur. Adult colugos are usually between 14 and 17 inches (36–43 cm) long. They weigh between 2 and 4 pounds (1–2 kg).

The two species of colugos are alike in many ways. Both animals are about the size of a heavy squirrel. Both species

The flying lemur looks a lot like a squirrel. It has large eyes to help it see at night.

have pale fur on their undersides, with a mix of darker gray and brown fur on their backs. This coloring provides **camouflage** that helps the animal blend in with the bark on tree trunks.

Time to Glide!

Some people think colugos look like bats when they glide. Colugos even have webs between their fingers, as do bats. Bats have extra long finger bones, though.

When flying lemurs want to move from one tree to another, they spread their arms and legs and glide. A piece of furry skin called the patagium stretches along each side of a flying lemur's body. It connects the animals' necks, front legs, back legs, and tails. This skin catches the air in much the

Flying lemurs use the flaps of skin that stretch from their hands to their feet and to their tails to catch the air. The patagium is thin and stretchy.

same way that the wings on a paper airplane do. Flying lemurs can glide up to 230 feet (70 m) before landing on a new branch.

Colugos move slowly on the ground. This makes them easy for **predators** to catch. Because of this, colugos do not come down to the ground often.

It's a Fact!

1

The Sunda flying lemur is named for the Sunda Islands. These islands are part of the Southeast Asian countries of Indonesia, Malaysia, and Brunei.

4

Philippine flying lemurs often live near farms that grow coconut trees or rubber trees.

5

Colugos often eat while hanging upside down!

2

Some scientists who have studied Sunda flying lemurs from different islands think this species should be separated into two or more species

3

The camouflaging fur on Sunda flying lemurs has brighter patches of color than does the fur of the Philippine flying lemur. These bright patches look like the **lichen** that grows on the trees in its habitat.

6

Scientists once thought that colugos ate insects, as do many other small mammals. Studies of their teeth showed that colugos eat only plants, though.

7

In some parts of Southeast Asia, people hunt flying lemurs for their meat.

8

Fruit farmers consider flying lemurs pests because they eat the farmers' crops.

Up in the Trees

Because their arms are not that strong, they do not move quickly through the trees, unless they are gliding.

Most flying lemurs are **solitary**. This means that they live alone. Some may live in small, loosely connected groups, though. Each colugo can be **territorial** about the places it sleeps and likes to find food.

Colugos use their claws to climb up tree trunks and to hang from branches. They are better gliders than they are climbers, though!

How does a colugo move between the trees in its range? First, it uses its sharp claws to hold on to and climb a tree trunk. It climbs slowly using small hops. When it wants to move to another tree, it climbs to a nice high spot. Then it jumps out from a branch and spreads its arms and legs and glides to the next tree. It does this over and over to move across a forest.

15

Looking for Food

Colugos are **herbivores**, or animals that eat only plants. They eat shoots, flowers, sap, and fruits from the different trees in their habitat. They eat mostly the leafy parts of trees, though. When they get hungry, colugos glide to a well-liked feeding place within their range. When they find

Flying lemurs eat many kinds of plants, including the leaves on palm trees.

Here a colugo uses its tongue to lick plant matter from a branch.

a leafy branch, they use their front feet to pull it close. Then they use their lower teeth to scrape the leaves. Their lower front teeth are well suited to this job. They have a comblike shape and each tooth has up to 20 **tines**. After they scrape the leaves, colugos then use their large tongues to lick up the plant material.

Flying Lemur Predators

While colugos are eating plants, they must be on the lookout for predators such as the Philippine eagle. Colugos are slow moving, both in the trees and on the ground. They have a few ways they stay safe, though.

Philippine eagles, also called monkey-eating eagles, are one of the main predators of flying lemurs. They are some of the largest, most powerful birds in the world.

One way colugos avoid predators is to stay high in the treetops, away from most other animals. Another way that colugos avoid predators is by sitting very still. Their fur

Flying lemurs try to stay very still if there is a predator nearby. If the predator spots them, then they will jump and glide to another tree.

camouflages them, letting them blend in with tree bark. Finally, if a predator gets too close, colugos can jump from that tree and glide to escape.

Baby Colugos

Male and female flying lemurs come together to have babies throughout the year. Colugo young grow inside the mothers for about 60 days. There is usually only one baby born at a time, although sometimes a female will give birth to twins.

Flying lemurs hold their babies in the pocket formed by the patagium when it is folded up. They can fold it on their stomachs or on their backs.

A newborn colugo is very small and completely helpless when it is born. The mother must carry her young at all times, even while gliding! To hold her young, the mother folds the bottom part

Babies hang on tight to their mothers' stomachs for their first few months.

of her patagium into a warm little pocket to hold her young against her stomach. The mother nurses her young for about six months. Colugos reach their adult size at between two and three years of age.

Flying Lemurs and Habitat Loss

Flying lemurs are not **endangered**, but their numbers have been going down as people cut down forests. This leads to habitat loss for flying lemurs. Habitat loss means that colugos and other animals need to compete with each other for food and places to live. The good news is that some forests in Southeast Asia are not allowed to be cut down. This keeps these places safe as habitats for animals like the colugo.

Colugos count on their forest habitats to stay alive.

Nearly everything we know about colugos comes from studying them in their natural habitat. Scientists have had trouble keeping colugos alive in captivity. This means that there is still much to be learned about these fascinating little animals.

Glossary

arboreal (ahr-BOR-ee-ul) Having to do with trees.

camouflage (KA-muh-flahj) A color or shape that matches what is around something and helps hide it.

endangered (in-DAYN-jerd) In danger of no longer living.

habitats (HA-buh-tats) The surroundings where animals or plants naturally live.

herbivores (ER-buh-vorz) Animals that eat only plants.

lichen (LY-ken) A living things that is made of two kinds of living things, called an alga and a fungus.

mammals (MA-mulz) Warm-blooded animals that have backbones and hair, breathe air, and feed milk to their young.

nocturnal (nok-TUR-nul) Active during the night.

predators (PREH-duh-terz) Animals that kill other animals for food.

primates (PRY-mayts) The group of animals that are more advanced than others and includes monkeys, gorillas, and people.

solitary (SAH-leh-ter-ee) Spending most time alone.

species (SPEE-sheez) One kind of living thing. All people are one species.

territorial (ter-uh-TAWR-ee-ul) Having to do with land or space that animals guard for their use.

tines (TYNZ) Thin, pointed parts.

tropical (TRAH-puh-kul) Warm year-round.

Index

Web Sites

Due to the changing nature of Internet links, PowerKids Press has developed an online list of Web sites related to the subject of this book. This site is updated regularly. Please use this link to access the list:
www.powerkidslinks.com/uptr/lemur/